THE HAPPY
MINIMALIST

The Happy
Minimalist

FINANCIAL INDEPENDENCE,
GOOD HEALTH,
AND A BETTER PLANET FOR US ALL

Peter Lawrence

Front cover picture: Author's living room

To order additional copies of this book, contact:
Xlibris Corporation
1-888-795-4274
www.Xlibris.com
Orders@Xlibris.com
49829

CONTENTS

This book is dedicated to

My family
You were definitely instrumental in shaping me to become a minimalist. It is time you yourselves consider becoming minimalists.

My friends
You encouraged me to write this book. Well, here it is. Enjoy reading it, and become part of the "minimalist movement" in your own way and time.

My fellow minimalists
I hope this book will further affirm your lifestyles.

Minimalist wannabes
I hope this book will win you over.

The remaining majority
I know I won't be able to change your minds and hence your lifestyles. Nevertheless, I hope you will pick up some useful nuggets of information.

GENESIS: HOW THIS BOOK CAME ABOUT

On May 4, 2007, my doctor looked at my blood test results and ordered me to go on medication immediately for my high cholesterol. I suggested that perhaps I should try adjusting my diet and lifestyle first. But she dismissed that idea and wrote me a prescription for simvastatin (20 mg). I went to the pharmacy and asked them for the literature on this drug and reviewed it, paying close attention to the side effects. I then went to a quiet place and contemplated on whether I should adhere to my doctor's advice. Several minutes later, I decided I was not going to depend on any pharmaceutical company to help bring my cholesterol level down. For the most part, I have lived a life that is drug-free, prescribed or otherwise. It had worked well for me and I wanted to continue that. If once upon a time my cholesterol level was normal, I was confident that I could bring it back to a normal level again. I did not want the pharmaceutical companies to profit at my expense. I decided that I would try to bring it down naturally via diet and lifestyle changes. I went to the library and borrowed several books related to cholesterol and started reading them. I planned a regimen of diet and lifestyle based on whatever I had distilled from various sources. I became confident that I would have my cholesterol level under control within a few months. I also decided that once I had successfully brought it down, I would write a book on how I did it. Months later, the blood test revealed that my cholesterol level did drop—by a whopping 22 percent! I also lost about eight pounds, although this was never my intention. The best part was that I lost it at the right place, too—around my abs. I felt vindicated. I started to make plans for writing the book. As I did a survey on the interest level in such a book, it dawned on me that a solution in a pill was more palatable than a book prescribing changes to diet and lifestyle.

Someone planted the idea in my head of writing instead about my "unique minimalist lifestyle." I shared the idea of the book *The Minimalist* and received considerable support. One person said, "I envy you, as you know how to live and be happy without stuff."

Over the years, several friends, colleagues, and even some bosses had commented that I had a lot to contribute but never seemed to share my knowledge or experience. I decided to take this opportunity to address that. As part of this book, I have included a section called "Ethical Will" (appendix G). Ethical will is a way of leaving behind something more meaningful than material goods. I am not going to live forever. And even during my lifetime, I may not have the opportunity to share my knowledge and experience. Including this section provides a means to share my "values" not only with people I know, but also those I have yet to know. Now, no one can accuse me of not sharing my knowledge!

There are at least two reasons we suffer: because of our own mistakes and because of the mistakes of others. If I drive under the influence of alcohol and consequently crash and am paralyzed for life, that was my mistake. If someone else was drunk and rear-ended me, consequently incapacitating me, that is what I call suffering because of the mistake of others. As you can see, it is not sufficient that we alone are educated, enlightened, and disciplined. It is in our own best interest to ensure others are, as well. The current mortgage crisis demonstrates clearly that the greed or ignorance of some can have grave implications on the entire nation. So this book is an attempt to share with as many people as possible the benefits of the lifestyle of a minimalist. I strongly believe that many people would have been able to avert many of the predicaments they are in today if the lifestyle advocated in this book had been followed. If much of what I have to say here is not new to you, I hope it will at least serve as a reminder. By putting it out there, I am also subjecting myself to scrutiny. I am sure you will help keep me honest.

Although I am writing this book as a single guy, that does not make it irrelevant for others. If you are in a relationship, it will do both sides good to simplify your lives before you get into longer term commitments together. Clutter on your end and clutter on your future spouse's end, only add to more clutter and complications. For already married couples, it is never too late to start. Even though I don't have any children at the moment, I seem to be more concerned about what sort of planet we will be leaving our future generations. I am surprised that many couples with children aren't at least as concerned. The daily choices we make have implications on our future progeny.

I hope that reading this book will help you with the following:

1. Realize that more is not necessarily better. Beyond a certain point, "more" becomes detrimental.
2. Understand that just because you can afford something does not necessarily mean that you should acquire it. There are social, environmental, and other considerations beyond the mere financial.
3. Become aware that there are alternatives to what is thought to be right or proper.

4. Ask yourself the right questions to help you arrive at what is really important and what really matters.
5. Recognize the possible excesses in your current lifestyle and be motivated to eliminate them.
6. Believe that seemingly insignificant actions on your part, over time and when repeated by other individuals, can have a phenomenal impact.

In the spirit of its title, I have attempted to keep the contents of this book as succinct as possible. I have avoided going into details and have limited myself to just presenting a wealth of ideas, questions, and possibilities. I hope that some of the terms or notions mentioned in this book pique your interest enough to do further reading.

Disclaimer: I am not a doctor, nor am I a certified financial planner.

WHAT IS A MINIMALIST?

The *Compact Oxford English Dictionary* explains it as:

1.   an advocate or practitioner of minimal art or music
2.   an advocate of moderate political reform.

My scope of a minimalist is broader than the typical dictionary definition. I describe a minimalist as a person who minimizes everything and anything to what is absolutely necessary. According to Greek philosopher Epicurus, whose thinking encapsulates my view, the troubles entailed by maintaining an extravagant lifestyle tend to outweigh the pleasure of enjoying that lifestyle. He recommended that what was necessary for life and happiness be maintained at minimal cost, believing that anything beyond what is necessary should either be tempered by moderation or completely avoided.

I had arrived at this same conclusion myself, independent of this ancient Athenian philosopher. Apparently, many people past and present have arrived at similar conclusions, too. Clearly, the concept or idea is not novel. The challenge is how many of us actually do succeed in living the life of a minimalist and are happy and content.

Two common misconceptions need to be dispelled. The first is that minimalists lead depressed or deprived lives. This is not true. (I hope what is said about me on the back cover of this book convinces you.) The second misconception is that minimalists are stingy or cheap. The truth is that minimalists do spend. But they are focused on what, how, and when they expend their resources. Remember that it is not just money we are talking about here. It is everything we have at our disposal: time, money, food, effort, thoughts, etc. If anything, the minimalist can be accused of being an efficiency nut, because he tries to maximize any and all resources he has.

Let me illustrate this point by an example on the practice of giving presents at Christmas. In general, people spend a lot more on presents than those gifts are worth to the recipients. Joel Waldfogel, an economist at the University of Pennsylvania calls this phenomenon "the deadweight loss of Christmas." A deadweight loss is created, for example, when you spend one hundred dollars to give someone a sweater that he or she values at only, say, ninety dollars. The ten dollar difference then becomes the deadweight loss. If you extrapolate that to the billions of dollars spent by everyone—not only on Christmas but all other "special" occasions—billions of dollars are lost every year. What is the alternative to this "waste"? One approach the minimalist would take is to give only what is needed to whoever needs it most. Example: During Christmas season, Christmas-giving trees are set up at various locations—with cards hanging from them that display what a child wants. Let's say one of the cards comes from a nine-year-old boy asking for a school uniform. A minimalist would spend the money buying a school uniform (or two) for this boy he does not know, rather than buying a toy, say, for his nephew. In the mind of the minimalist, the boy needs the uniform more than his nephew needs the toy. A minimalist is not stingy. A minimalist is merely judicious in how he spends his money. Another example: If the minimalist had to choose between locally and organically grown vegetables in season or frozen conventionally grown vegetables from abroad, the minimalist will choose the former even though it may cost more. A minimalist is prepared to pay the premium to do what is right.

In economics, the law of diminishing marginal utility states that as a person increases consumption of a product (while keeping consumption of other products constant); there is a decline in the marginal utility that a person derives from consuming each additional unit of that product. A common example used to illustrate this law is when you're hungry and yearn for a burger. The first burger you eat will yield tremendous satisfaction. Let's say you decide to have a second one; even though you are paying the same price for it, you will not get the same level of satisfaction you got from the first burger. Each additional consumption decreases your satisfaction or utility. Using this law, I have developed this notion of upr (utility per resource). The chart below helps depict the notion. The first thing to note is that beyond the optimum point, any further resource utilized follows the law of diminishing marginal utility. When you are not aware of where the optimum point is, you unwittingly go on utilizing resources ("I can afford it" mentality), thinking that you are gaining more satisfaction ("More is better" mentality). If this behavior goes unchecked, it leads to a point where the utility goes negative, meaning it does you harm (e.g. overeating can lead to obesity).

One way to summarize this notion: When you get past the optimum point, you are better off diverting the resource elsewhere. If not, you are not maximizing your resource. Once you go to the negative territory, it is no longer just a case of not maximizing your resource; it is a case of disservice to yourself and others. The minimalist is aware of these consequences and always tries to determine the optimum point. The minimalist is disciplined enough to divert resources beyond the optimum point to where there is better return. (Note that the numbers used in the chart are arbitrary to help convey the concept. It is not always possible or easy to accurately determine the optimum point. In some cases like vehicle fuel efficiency, a similar chart could be determined scientifically by looking at mpg versus mph. In other cases, it is more subjective.)

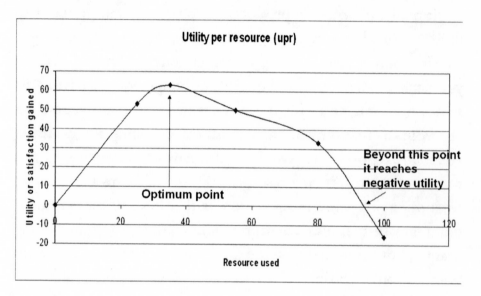

Key points

- A minimalist lifestyle does not mean no spending or limited spending. It means eliminating spending resources on wasteful endeavors and instead directing the resources toward initiatives that add true value.
- A minimalist not only considers the financial impact of his or her decision but is also conscientious about the social and environmental impact of decisions.

PETER LAWRENCE

-   A minimalist considers the short-term as well as the long-term implications of decisions.

There is also a range of minimalism. On one end of the spectrum, you have perhaps someone like Chris McCandless, who gave up his entire life savings and ventured into the wild. Each of us has to find our own niche in this scale.

WARM-UP

The purpose of this section is to get you warmed up to various perspectives of life and what is important. We start with a song, followed by dialogue from a movie. Following that are some quotes from luminaries and finally a question for you to think about and answer.

Below are parts of the lyrics from the song "Soak up the Sun." It was originally performed by Sheryl Crow.

> I don't have digital
> I don't have diddly squat
> It's not having what you want
> It's wanting what you've got
>
> I'm gonna soak up the sun
> I'm gonna tell everyone to lighten up
> I'm gonna tell 'em that
> I've got no one to blame
> For every time I feel lame
> I'm looking up
> I'm gonna soak up the sun
> While it's still free
> I'm gonna soak up the sun
> Before it goes out on me

Here is dialogue from the movie "Lost Horizon":

Sondra Bizet: I saw a man whose life was empty. Oh I know it was full of this and full of that. But you were accomplishing nothing. You were going nowhere, and you knew it. As a matter of fact, all I saw was a little boy whistling in the dark.

Robert Conway: You're absolutely right. And I had to come all the way to a pigeon house in Shangri-La to find the only other person in the world who knew it. May I congratulate you?

Below are some quotes to review and ponder. I strongly encourage you to contemplate each of them and review them more than once if you have to.

We are happy in proportion to the things we can do without. (Henry David Thoreau)

Most of the luxuries, and many of the so-called comforts of life, are not only not indispensable, but positive hindrances to the elevation of mankind. With respect to luxuries and comforts, the wisest have even lived a more simple and meager life than the poor. (Henry David Thoreau)

Nature has enough to satisfy the needs of everyone but nothing to satisfy the greed of even a few. (Mahatma Gandhi)

Human suffering stems from desire. (Buddha)

I believe that a simple and unassuming manner of life is best for everyone, best both for the body and the mind. (Albert Einstein)

They came into this world naked, and when they die, they will be just as naked. They can't take anything with them, and they won't have anything to show for all their work. (Ecclesiastes 5:15)

The people asked John how they should live and John answered, if you have two coats, give one to someone who has none and if you have food, do the same. (Luke 3:10-11)

Life is really simple, but we insist on making it complicated. (Confucius)

Simplicity is the ultimate sophistication. (Leonardo da Vinci)

Have little and receive
Have much and be confused. (Lao Tzu)

How few our real wants, and how vast our imaginary ones. (John Casper Lavater)

Wise men count their blessings—fools their problems. (Anonymous)

I cried because I had no shoes until I saw the man who had no feet. (Unknown)

Contentment is natural wealth, luxury is artificial poverty. (Socrates)

An Abundance mentality springs from internal security, not from external rankings, comparisons, opinions, possessions, or associations. (Stephen R. Covey)

When you don't have something, your only problem is that you don't have it. When you have it, it brings together with it a lot of headaches such as maintaining it, protecting it etc. When you lose it, your headaches will turn to heartache. (My mom)

Now for a "camping" question: Think about the time you went camping that yielded the best, most joyful experience for you. What was it that made it joyful?

Was there anything you would rather have had to make the experience even more joyful? Note down your answers.

WHY BE A MINIMALIST?

Before we go further, have you asked yourself why you are not a minimalist? Have you ever wondered if your life was just like a hamster in a spinning wheel? The poor hamster keeps spinning and yet it does not make any progress. It remains exactly where it started, despite all its efforts. Talk about confusing activity with progress! Many of us go about our lives in the same way. We wake up, get ready for work, put up with whatever we have to put up with on the way to work, at work, and back from work. We return to the same grind the next day. For what, you wonder.

There are alternatives. You don't have to play this game—or at least, you don't have to play it the way it is played by most people. You can decide what success means to you instead of letting other people decide for you. All you need is some quality time to think it through.

> All men's miseries derive from not being able to sit in a
> quiet room alone. (Blaise Pascal)

Most people go about the lives without consciously and conscientiously thinking about them. The dreams of their parents influence them. The wishes of their spouses compel them. And the norms and practices of the world dictate their lifestyles. We think we are laboring for a good life. But what is "good" is both subjective and relative. Ask yourself the following questions:

1. If you were born in 1900 and were in a position to be able to afford everything you wanted at that time, will you have been happy?

   If the answer is yes, how many of the things that you have today, things you think are needed for your happiness, were not available then?

   If you could have been happy about a hundred years ago without them, why do you need them now to be happy?

   If you could be happy without them, then why are you laboring for those same things today?

2. Or imagine you were born in a war-torn country where you do not know where your next meal is coming from. What would you deem as a true need in that scenario?

The above questions should make you realize that a lot of what we think we need is dependent upon the time or circumstances we are in. They are not absolute nor are they universal. If we boil down to the basics, we only need the following to survive physically:

1. Fresh air
2. Clean water
3. Nutritious food
4. Adequate shelter (this includes clothes and anything to protect you from danger)

All else are wants, and in some cases luxuries.

(I am aware of Abraham Maslow's hierarchy of needs. I am focusing this discussion on universal physical needs.)

You will certainly not perish as long as you have all of the above. But if you have everything else you think you need, and even *one* of the above is missing, you will not survive long. Yet we are usually not satisfied with just the above and we crave for more. Over time, we begin to erroneously think that many of our wants are needs. Incessant advertising is used to brainwash us. A perceived need is created and a purchase is beckoned.

The fact of the matter is, if you want more, you will have to have the means to afford it. For many people, that literally translates to either working longer or working harder—or both. Even if you work smart, at the end of the day it is still work. If you enjoy what you are doing and you get paid for it, that's fantastic! However, is that true in your case? For many of us, we exchange our time, skills, labor, etc. for money. The more wants we have, the more time and resources we will have to invest to earn the money we need to satisfy the wants we desire. The good news is that the reverse can also be true. If you have fewer wants, you don't really have to work hard or long. You can escape from this spinning wheel you are in. By deliberately thinking about what you really need and want, you can spend more time and energy on the things you truly enjoy.

George Kinder, a financial planner and founder of the Kinder Institute of Life Planning, has a set of three questions famous for their ability to focus on what really matters:

Question 1: Imagine you have enough money to take care of your needs now and in the future. How would you live your life? Would you change anything?

Question 2: Imagine that your doctor says you have only five years to live. You won't feel sick, but you'll never know when death will come. What will you do? Will you change your life? How?

Question 3: Now imagine that your doctor says you have one day to live. Ask yourself—what did I miss? What did I not get to be or do?

Take some time to review the questions above and jot down your responses.

Once you have written the answers, ask yourself this question:

What prevents me right now from doing what I wanted to be or do?

Consider the following:

If you are not a student and you have bought this book, you are probably in the top two percent of the richest people in the world. Check it out for yourself at www.globalrichlist.com. Four billion people, or two-thirds of humanity, live on less than two dollars a day. Yes, our cost of living here is much higher. That is true. However, it is also true that you can live without many of the things you have come to believe you need.

Now let's look at some of the reasons to be a minimalist:

Good for your soul. Some of the quotes presented in the warm-up section earlier may remind you that many of the great souls voluntarily chose to lead simple lives. They were minimalists. Take Buddha as an example. He was a prince. He had several palaces and a beautiful wife. He gave up all that to find enlightenment.

> What benefit will it be to you if you gain the whole world
> but lose your own soul? (Mark 8:36)

Good for the society. In "Lost Horizon," the character Chang explains to the character George Conway why there is no crime in Shangri-La: "There can be no crime where there is a sufficiency of everything." In Shangri-La, sufficiency is possible because no one person has more than their neighbor. The challenge we have in the real world is the vast disparity between the haves and have-nots. This gap is not only within our own country but also extends between countries. If the gap continues to grow, at some point, unpleasant social consequences can result. The minimalist, even though he or she may be able to afford certain luxuries, avoids them (or at least minimizes them). This has two benefits:

1. It does not create a sense of "insufficiency" among the have-nots. They would not resent you.
2. It does not plow limited resources away from producing items that are necessary for basic survival.

Just because you can afford something should not exempt you from becoming a minimalist. Appendixes A and B provide more information for you to mull over.

Good for the country. We have an obesity epidemic. We also have a negative savings rate. It has been estimated that the annual cost of overweight and obesity in the United States is $122.9 billion (source: http://www.obesityinamerica.org). Most cases of obesity are caused by consuming more calories than the body expends. Being a minimalist and consuming less will be one step in the right direction. In a similar vein, we have a negative savings rate because we spend more than we earn. The mortgage crisis we are in is due to borrowers taking on more debt than they should and lenders extending more loans than they should. A nation of minimalists would not have run the country into the predicament we are in.

Cut your coat according to your cloth. (English proverb)

Good for the planet. Treading lightly on this planet and utilizing resources only when you absolutely have to leads to less wastage. The more energy you need means the more fossil fuels are used. This results in more carbon dioxide, which contributes to more global warming. A true minimalist uses less energy, hence minimizing the potential for climate change. The impact our lives have on the environment is mind-boggling:

- Though accounting for only 5 percent of the world's population, Americans consume 26 percent of the world's energy (source: *American Almanac*).

- If everyone in the world consumed like the average American, we'd need about six Earths to sustain ourselves.[i]
- To make all of the U.S. newspapers for one year, it takes 191,000,000 trees.[ii]
- Producing and disposing of all the junk mail distributed in the U.S. each year releases as much carbon dioxide as 2.8 million cars.[iii]

In February 2007, the Intergovernmental Panel on Climate Change indicated that warming caused by human activity was probably influencing other aspects of climate change, including a rise in the number of heat waves, extreme storms and droughts as well as ocean warming and wind. The Iroquois (American Indian) law required that decisions are made only after considering the impact it would have on the seventh generation. How many generations down the line do you think of when you make your decisions? If you are married with children, are you thinking about the sort of planet you will be leaving behind for your children and grandchildren?

Good for your pocketbook. A minimalist lifestyle lowers your cost of living. This in turn results in you not having to work long and hard. Often, people underestimate this fact. When you procure something, you should not only consider the initial list price. There are other costs to consider. A simple example to illustrate this point:

Assume both Tom and Dick are single and earn about $20/hour. Both have worked sufficient hours to take care of their four basic physical needs identified earlier. Tom is satisfied and is happy to take the weekend off. Dick is not totally satisfied because he has an eye on a flat panel high-definition TV listed at $1,000. How many more hours will Dick have to work in order to afford the flat panel HDTV? Most people will say fifty more hours. In truth, it is much more:

- List price of HD TV: $1,000
- Sales tax (8.25% in California) = $82.5
- Total with sales tax = $1,082.50

Given the tax rate schedule, Dick will probably fall in the 25 percent tax bracket. Hence, in order to afford the TV, the salary he will need to earn is: $1,082.5/ (100%-25%) = $1443.33.

In order to earn $1,443.33, Dick will need to work slightly more than seventy-two hours. In the above example, I have only considered federal tax. If you consider state tax, Social Security, etc., the impact will be greater. In some cases, you will need to consider the following:

1. Maintenance costs (e.g., warranty or protection plan, insurance).
2. Cost for accessories such as cables, furniture to hold your new item, etc.

Key points:

- You have to consider the total cost of ownership from the moment you own it till the time you dispose of it, including the cost of accessories you may end up buying.

- You have to consider the pretax dollars you will need to earn in order to afford it and not the list price alone.

After considering the above, the question that Dick will seriously have to ask himself is whether the extra hours he has to work are worth the joy the new flat panel TV is going to offer him. He will also need to consider the impact the extra hours will have on his mental and physical health as well as the impact it will have on his social life. Remember that the flat panel TV is probably not going to last him a lifetime.

Perhaps Dick is more prepared than Tom to put in the extra hours. As willing as he is, he may make a more informed choice if he knows that there is an alternative. He could save or invest his hard-earned money rather than spend it on the HDTV. Appendix D demonstrates the impact of saving and investing.

A penny saved is a penny earned. (Benjamin Franklin)

A French writer by the name of Diderot was given a fancy new gown, so he tossed his old one. Not long after, he realized that his desk was shabby compared to his new gown. So he got himself a new desk. Next it was the tapestry and then the curtains and so on till he replaced the entire contents of his study. This drive for consistency between possessions is known as the "Diderot effect." Have you been a victim of it? Would you be a victim of it again?

Good for your mental health. Minimizing what you have forces you to be creative. It nudges you to use what you already have to achieve similar results. Personally, I try not to have any single-function devices or appliances. I challenge myself to *create* a solution instead of *purchase* a solution.

Some simple teasers for you:

If you have a VCR but don't have a TV, can you still use the VCR to watch video cassette tapes?

Could you use something you already have in your house without having to buy a computer desk for your notebook computer?

Good for your physical health. Exercise gets embedded into your way of life when you don't have certain luxuries. Imagine you opted for a car that doesn't have some modern convenience, like power windows. What would it force you to do? As trivial as it may seem, small things add up. I remember reading about a big shot who always had people opening his door for him; at some point when he had to open his own door, he could not do it. "Use it or lose it" applies to many of our faculties. When I was in New Mexico, I visited Taos Pueblo. The pueblo is actually many individual homes built side by side with common walls but no connecting doorways. In earlier days, entry was gained only from the top using a ladder. When a tourist asked how elderly people managed, the tour guide smiled and said that the very action of having to regularly use the ladder helped prevent the faculties from degenerating.

Exposure to chemicals used in some flame retardants may pose health risks.[iv] Since some of our furniture has flame retardants, more furniture means more possibility of the presence of flame retardants. Some states are considering banning them.

Minimizing your calories is good for your health. In the book *The Longevity Diet*, the author shows that calorie restriction is the only proven way to slow the aging process and maintain peak vitality.

Health or wealth? At the end of the day, you will have to decide what you can live with and what you can live without. You will have to consider carefully the implication of wanting something. If you have more wants, you will have to accumulate more wealth to be able to afford them. There is no point spending most of your lifetime accumulating wealth at the expense of your health only to spend that wealth later in trying to restore your health.

Easy to maintain. The fewer things you have, the easier it is to maintain them. Fewer pieces of unnecessary furniture translates to less dusting and cleaning of those pieces.

Easy to find. The fewer things you have, the easier it is to find things. The more cluttered your space is, the harder and longer it is going to take you to find something.

Easy to move. On January 2005, I moved back to Santa Clara, California, from Houston, Texas. I did not get any movers to move my things nor did I have to rent a U-haul truck or van. I put everything I had into my Honda Civic and did a road trip back to California. Right now, I have all my essential stuff (documents and extra cash) in one backpack. If I have one minute to leave my place, I can just grab that bag and go. If I have one hour, I can pack all my belongings into my car and drive off.

Your personal efficiency improves. A car is considered more efficient when it can go more miles with less fuel. Just like when you look at mpg (miles per gallon) of a vehicle to gauge its fuel efficiency, you should look at your own upr (utility per resource). How much resource do you utilize to keep yourself going? If you can get a higher or the same level of satisfaction or utility from less resource, aren't you by definition more efficient?

HOW TO BECOME A MINIMALIST

Phase One: Minimize Things (or Consume Less)

1. Identify what you don't need.

    You can start with what you have not used a single time in the past twelve months. If you survived without using it over that time, chances are that you don't really need it. I use twelve months as a measure to cater to the different seasons. Of course, there are logical exceptions to the above rule such as tools, fire extinguishers and emergency supplies (which hopefully you will never have to use). Ask yourself this question: If something is not useful or joyful to me, what is the reason I should hang on to it? Take a look at all the books you have. Review each of them and ask yourself, "When was the last time I read this?" Consider selling them or donating them to your local library. If they continue to sit on your shelf, they only take up space and collect dust. Passing them on will yield some utility to someone else. This consequently improves the upr of a city or nation.

2. Relook at some of the things you think you need, to ensure that you really need them. I will give a simple example which I believe will be applicable to you. Many people buy water filters. We think we need them. If you study what the water filters actually remove and what is actually contained in your water source, you may realize that many chemicals the water filter

can remove are not present in the water supply to begin with. I studied the cover of one faucet water filter and it claimed it reduces the following: 2,4-D; silvex, alachlor; asbestos; atrazine; benzene; carbofuran; carbon tetrachloride; chlordane, cysts; endrin; ethylbenzene; heptachlor epoxide; lead; lindane; mercury; methoxychlor; monochlorobenzene; MTBE; o-dichlorobenzene; simazine; styrene; tetrachloroethene; toluene; trichloroethene; TTHMs; toxaphene; turbidity. I then cross-checked this list with the city's published water quality table and found that none of the above were listed in the table. If that is the case, is there any point in purchasing the filter? To be absolutely sure, I wrote to the City to check if their testing revealed any of the above chemicals. I got the following reply: "We have not detected any of the chemicals you listed in the City's well water." (The compliance manager for the Water and Sewer Utilities for my city was extremely patient with all the questions that I asked and answered them promptly and professionally.) This is a simple but real example to illustrate that we may be paying for things that we don't really need. (Don't assume that since I don't need a water filter, you don't need one. Cross-check like I did.)

3. Get rid of what you identified above.
    You can get rid of it by doing the following:

    a. Selling whatever you can (Amazon, Craigslist, eBay).
    b. Donating items to those who actually need them. If you don't know anyone who needs your items, there are always the Goodwill stores and Salvation Army stores.

c. Recycling what you cannot sell or donate.

4. Start enjoying your newfound luxury:

    a. You have more space.
    b. You have more money (proceeds from any sale you made).
    c. You feel good (you donated items to those who needed them more than you).
    d. You did your part in preserving the planet (you recycled).
    e. You made your house safer: By minimizing clutter, you minimized fuel to fire. The fewer things you have also means fewer things falling when there is an earthquake.
    f. Better luck? For those who believe in feng shui: The exercise you just performed helped remove clutter and clutter is bad feng shui. Clutter blocks the smooth flow of chi through your space and weighs you down energetically. By removing clutter, you have facilitated the smooth flow of energy.

Phase Two: Minimize Services

1. Identify services you don't really need and get rid of those totally or pare down.
    Here are examples:

    a. Landline: Do you really need a traditional telephone line or can you manage with just a cell phone?

b. Cell phone: What plan do you have? Do you know how many minutes you generally use every month? Are you paying more for what you really need?

c. Do you really need satellite dish or cable? Can you survive with good old "rabbit ears" antenna (dipole antenna)? Satellite dish and cable companies tout proudly the vast number of channels they offer. I find that amusing because it is not the quantity that matters. It is the quality of the programs available that should matter. If you are selective in what you watch, you don't really need two hundred channels, do you? Wouldn't you rather have one channel that broadcasts the programs that interest you rather than a few hundred channels most of which broadcast junk? Is there a way to just watch only what you want and if needed just pay for only that?

d. How much do you pay for electricity every month? I pay about $12. I will share how I achieve that in a later section. You can start by replacing incandescent bulbs with compact fluorescent bulbs. A compact fluorescent lamp uses 70 to 80 percent less electricity and lasts 10 to 13 times longer than an incandescent bulb.

Phase Three: Minimize Routines

We perform several activities usually for one of following reasons:

a. That is the way it has always been done (tradition)
b. That is the way people do it (culture)

    c. Because it feels good (emotion)

    d. Because I have to (obligation)

Well, it is time to question tradition, challenge pop culture, check your emotion, and revise your obligations. Consider the following:

1. Are you attending something because your father, grandfather, and great-grandfather attended it? Do you find it useful or joyful? Do other people benefit or derive joy by your attendance? If the answer is no to both, why bother attending?

2. How many times in a week or month do you do grocery shopping or do your laundry? Any chance of reducing it? Are we washing our clothes more than necessary? If you had to wash by hand, would you still be washing some of your clothes that frequently? Is convenience leading us to perform superfluous tasks?

3. How many dishes do you normally cook per meal? From the nutrition point of view, is there any reason to cook the number of dishes that you cook?

4. How many hours do you spend watching TV? Does it relax you or does the news depress you and the advertisements leave you wanting more?

Phase Four: Minimize New Acquisitions

Before you decide to consume or add new things, services, or routines, stop and question yourself about whether you really need it. Some people may suggest having this as the first phase. It is up to you. I put it here because your experience from the first three phases will have revealed a lot to you. Hopefully it will help you make better procurement decisions moving forward. Here are some further considerations and suggestions:

a. If you were to stop buying today, how long would the things you already possess last?

b. Will you outlive the things you have or will they outlive you? If it is the latter, what is the point in further acquisition?

c. Instead of buying it, could you repair what you have by bringing it to your local tailor or cobbler? When you do that, you not only potentially save money, you definitely reduce waste. You are also supporting a local small business owner. If you decide to go ahead and buy something new instead, which is branded and from a big company, most of the profits the company makes goes to reward the guys at the top. (Have a look at appendix B and decide for yourself the best course of action.) Purchasing something new also contributes to the depletion of limited natural resources and an increased carbon footprint.

Phase Five: Indulge in Extreme Sports

This is the phase I am in. I still have a ways to go. The path to simplification never ends. You keep challenging yourself to live with even less. One's heart rate at rest is usually between 60 and 80 beats per minute. Those who are physically fit tend to have a resting heart rate that is lower. You see, when you are aerobically fit, your heart becomes more efficient. It can pump the same amount of blood per minute by working less, hence the lower heart rate. In the same vein, in this phase you aspire to improve your personal efficiency—to use less resource to achieve satisfaction (utility). You explore the possibility of reaching the optimum level of satisfaction sooner so that you are free to divert any resource beyond the optimum point to other initiatives. The chart below should help drive home this point.

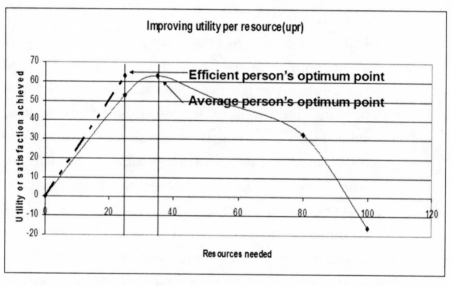

A tangible benefit of improving your upr is that doing so hastens your financial independence. For example, assume Tom and Dick both have an after-tax income of $3,500. Assume that Tom is an aspiring minimalist and only needs $2,500 a month while Dick may need $3,500 a month. Since Tom reaches his utility level with less resource, he is able to divert the remaining capital ($1,000)

to an investment that generates passive income for him. You will note in the chart that the curve of the minimalist does not extend beyond the optimum point, because he diverts the resource to fulfill some other utility. Between Tom and Dick, who do you think is going to be able to retire sooner? Feel free to check out appendix D to see the impact of savings and investments. Note that Tom is no less happy (or satisfied) than Dick is. Remember the hamster in the spinning wheel? Just as one should not confuse activity with results, one should be careful not to confuse more spending with more happiness (or utility). More resources—whether it is money, time, or energy—would only improve your utility till the optimum point. Beyond that, expending further resource has no benefit, as illustrated in the chart. If you are still not convinced by my layman's explanation, feel free to do your own reading around "threshold hypothesis," developed by Manfred Max-Neef. It is the notion that when macroeconomic systems expand beyond a certain size, the additional cost of growth exceeds the flow of additional benefits.

Allow me to end with an Aesop fable called "The Woman and Her Hen":

> A woman possessed a hen that gave her an egg every day. She often pondered how she might obtain two eggs daily instead of one, and at last, to gain her purpose, determined to give the hen a double allowance of barley. From that day the hen became fat and sleek, and never once laid another egg.

MY WAY

When friends visit me, they are shocked by the lack of furniture. However, every one of them who knows me personally will testify that I am extremely happy with the way I live. I do walk the talk. I will share with you now how I live the life of a minimalist. It is not the only way. It is just one way.

WARNING: It may seem too ascetic for some. In truth, once you have lived it, it is really not as bad as it may seem. You will just need to be a wee bit adventurous. Our preconceived notion of what a good life constitutes or what a good standard of living should be colors a lot of how we choose to lead our lives. Suspend that temporarily.

Bed. I don't have a bed. (No danger of falling from bed.) I consider my sleeping bag my bed. I have a liner that I use with the sleeping bag so that I only need to wash the liner regularly instead of the entire sleeping bag. I do have pillows. Cuddling up in my sleeping bag is fun and very comfortable especially in the winter. People say a firm mattress is important. Can you get firmer than the floor? GW, a friend of mine, has gotten used to sleeping on a firm mattress such that when he travels on business, he finds the hotel beds uncomfortable since they are too soft. He told me he usually ends up sleeping on the floor instead. I laughed and told him: "Well, that's how I sleep every day at home." As drastic as it may sound, it is really not as bad as you think. For couples, there are even sleeping bags made for two where you and your partner can snuggle comfortably. With the regular bed setup—you have the bed frame, box spring, and mattress to begin with. Some people will also want a headboard. Then you have sheets, comforter, etc., etc. You can replace all that hassle with a sleeping bag. You will be thankful when it comes to moving—especially when you have to move by yourself. One weekend when I still had the regular bed, like most people do, I decided to rearrange the position of my bed in my bedroom. As I was moving my queen-size mattress, I lost my balance and fell together with the mattress. As I was lying on the floor with the heavy mattress on top of me, I could only laugh, thinking about the "Seinfeld" episode where Elaine tries to move the mattress and falls pretty much in the same position as I did. I was fortunate. Unlike Elaine, I did not hurt my back. Recall the "camping question" that was posed in the warm-up section? Do you need to have a bed to experience joy?

TV. I don't have what people many people will consider as TV. My notebook computer acts as my TV. I have a USB TV tuner that I connect to my notebook computer. I have also connected my VCR to the USB TV tuner. (VCR may seem passé and it is. However, our public libraries still carry video cassettes. Not all titles can be found in DVD format.) With this setup, I can watch not only TV but also video cassettes and DVDs. I also have a projector that I use occasionally to view movies. My notebook computer is connected to a two-way PC speaker system that includes a subwoofer. I am totally pleased with the audio quality.

TiVo. Don't subscribe to it. I can record anything I want with the configuration I described earlier.

Satellite dish/cable. I don't subscribe to any. I use dipole antenna to get whatever broadcasts it can catch. For the rest, I depend on the Web. These days, many TV shows can be found on the respective Web sites anyway. If they are not there, some kind soul posts it on www.youtube.com. The following sites also offer free movies and TV shows:

> www.hulu.com
> www.joost.com

If you cannot find the shows you want for free, there are always paid alternatives:

> www.itunes.com
> www.vudu.com
> www.amazon.com/unbox

With this model, you only pay for what you want to watch instead of paying for several channels that you hardly use. You do not have to be a hostage to the cable and satellite companies, who raise their monthly charges whenever they want. They can do that because they know you are a captive audience. No pun intended!

Netflix or Blockbuster or other monthly movie rentals. Movies that I did not catch at the theaters, I may get at the public library. If I cannot get them there, I keep a list of movies that I want to watch. When either Netflix or Blockbuster try to get me to come back again through special offers, I go back just for that month and catch up on all the movies I want to watch. I maximize my month's subscription. No movie sits in the house for days. I do a quick turnaround. Being very selective in what I watch minimizes the number of movies I watch over time. You save time and money that can be invested for better use.

Dining table. None.

Computer table/desk. None. I use the ironing board that was left by the previous owner. As you may know, the ironing board allows you to adjust its height. So you can adjust it to a height that it is ergonomic as possible.

Sofa. None. I have foldable chairs. Don't worry. You don't have to sit on the floor if you happen to visit me.

Telephone landline. None. Cell phone is sufficient for me.

Cell phone. I have the lowest plan possible offered by the carrier. My monthly charge is usually less than $35. I don't subscribe to a data plan. I tell all my friends not to text message me. I encourage them to call me instead. This not only saves me money, but apparently it is also good for your brain. Dr. Ryuta Kawashima, who developed the game Brain Age, advises that one must seize every opportunity for discussion by engaging in direct conversation with many people every day. In this way, you will be forced to use words and gestures that stimulate the brain.

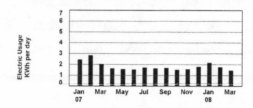

Service Type	Read Dates From	Read Dates To	Days	Meter Readings Current	Meter Readings Prior	Mult	Usage	Meter Number	Rate	This Month This Year (Daily Avg)	This Month Last Year (Daily Avg)
E	02/06	03/04	27	17500	17460	1	40 kWh	24695	D1	1 kWh	2 kWh

Electricity costs. As you can see from my bill, my daily electric usage never exceeds three kilowatts per hour. How can you achieve that? Here is how:

a. Slay the energy vampires. Turn off power and plug off adapters when not in use. Vampire load is a good example of wasted energy! You don't get any utility from it but you are still paying for it.

b. Consider replacing appliances with models that have the Energy Star ratings.

c. Replace incandescent bulbs with compact fluorescent lightbulbs. If every American replaced just one old-fashioned incandescent bulb, it would be the environmental equivalent of removing two million cars from the road. This is a clear example of how a seemingly insignificant individual action, when multiplied by the vast population, can translate to significant impact.

d. I only turn on lights if I absolutely have to. I have my blinds open most of the time to let natural light in. At night, if I turn on the lights and leave my blinds open, people from outside get to see me more clearly than I can see them. (I have almost floor-to-ceiling windows in my bedroom and living room.) As such, I usually keep my lights off. I am able to do whatever I need to do utilizing the lights from the outside. I get to enjoy the city lights at night better when my lights are switched off. (I live on the sixth floor.) I turn on the lights only when it is absolutely necessary. I have a portable lamp that I use when I read. I bought that lamp in 1997 and have yet to replace the bulb. It is not only better for your eyes, it also saves energy. You can get more info on the lamp that I use from http://www.ott-lite.com.

e. Limited use of heater. Even during winter, I don't turn on my baseboard heaters. (If needed, I turn on a portable ceramic heater briefly.) Heaters tend to dry the surroundings. This makes it very uncomfortable—at least for me. Some people may suggest getting a humidifier to solve the "dry problem." But that means an extra device and the associated electricity charges to power it. An extra device means extra care. If you own a humidifier, you have to keep it clean to prevent the growth of bacteria and molds. The U.S. Consumer Product Safety Commission (CPSC) is alerting consumers to possible health hazards resulting from dirty room humidifiers. Bacteria and fungi often grow in the tanks of portable and console room humidifiers and can be released in the mist. Breathing dirty mist may cause lung problems ranging from flulike symptoms to serious infection. Check out the following Web site for more details: http://www.cpsc.gov/cpscpub/pubs/5046.html

The point I am trying to make is that by not turning on the heater to begin with, you can avoid the environment from getting drier and hence eliminate the need for a humidifier and its associated costs. By wearing layers and sock slippers, you can keep yourself comfortable indoors during winter without having to turn on the heater. Of course, I live in California and it may be more feasible for me and not necessarily for, say, someone in Wisconsin. (If you have to turn on your heater, you can consider at least reducing your thermostat by two degrees or more.) Our bodies are amazing. They adapt fairly well. I was born and raised on a tropical island. Despite that, I seem to withstand winter better than some of my friends who were born and raised in temperate zones. I believe, over time, by not turning on my heater, my body has acclimated to colder weathers. Consider this: How well can you see underwater? Probably not so well. There are sea gypsies in Thailand's Surin islands that have developed superior underwater vision. To discover if this was a learned or genetic behavior, Swedish scientist Anna Gislén has been training Swedish children. Within four to six months, they picked up the skill.[v] The human body and mind are amazing. By pushing the envelope a little each time, we can achieve amazing results. Why subject ourselves to that? Well, nobody can accurately predict what sort of weather patterns we will be experiencing in the next ten, twenty, or fifty years. We also cannot guarantee that we will have 24/7 access to technology or modern comforts to shield us from any adverse conditions. By deliberately restricting ourselves of certain comforts now, we can train our mind and body to adapt to withstand any adverse conditions later. Think of it as a form of immunization.

Plan for difficulty while it is easy.

Manage the great while it's small. (Lao Tzu)

Consider the following scenario: One very cold winter, an earthquake or other natural catastrophe hits your town and you are out of power. No electricity! No heat! No lights! If you have already "trained" your body and mind to live in such conditions, life will go on pretty much as normal for you. Consider how you will handle such a scenario if you have not experienced life without the comforts of a heater or electricity. This is not a far-fetched scenario. If you have not already heard about such incidents, here are just two:

- In 2005, about 6 million Floridians were without power after hurricane Wilma plowed across the peninsula.
- In 2003, major power outages struck simultaneously across dozens of cities in the eastern United States and Canada. (Get another perspective of this incident at http://www.endofsuburbia.com/preview2.htm.)

I have heard that we waste more energy than we actually use. Either because of our ignorance or arrogance ("I can afford it" mind-set), we waste energy. If we became careful about it, we may not need to spend resources to build as many power generators. Ever wondered how many power generators are actually needed just to power wasted energy? Examples of wasted energy would include energy lost because of phantom loads or unwittingly leaving the lights on. Remember it is cheaper to conserve energy than to generate energy. Conserving energy can come in two ways: One by technology. The compact fluorescent lightbulbs are a good example. They can provide equal or better lighting for far less power. However, technology may take some time before it can reach the masses at cost-effective prices. In the absence of technology or while waiting for technology, you can still do something today: Conserve by using less power.

Cost of gas. I fill up my car with gas about two times a month and it comes to less than $40 a month. Why such minimal costs? Well, for the following reasons:

Minimal driving. My annual mileage on my car hovers around four thousand miles. If I can walk, I walk instead of driving. In some cases, I even take the train. Besides the financial aspect, driving less also helps to minimize the impact exhaust pollution has on the environment and health. Another sobering consideration: Minimizing driving also minimizes your chances of dying in an automobile accident. I remember some people being afraid to fly after 9/11 where about three thousand people died. Do you know how many people die in traffic-related deaths in the United States?[vi] About forty thousand. This is not an anomaly or a one-time event of forty thousand deaths. It is something that happens every year in the United States. Globally, the number is around 1.2 million.

Getting a more efficient car. I drive a 1999 Honda Civic. The mpg on it is pretty good. I also follow the regular maintenance on the car. Once I have fully utilized this car and need to get another car, it will definitely be a hybrid. By that time, the mpg will be much better than what we have in the hybrids today.

Maintaining your car well. This includes regular maintenance such as oil change and correct tire pressure. For every 6 psi the tire is underinflated, the fuel consumption increases by one percent.

Driving smart. When I see the traffic light turning amber several hundred feet away and there is no chance I can beat the red light, I usually will remove my leg from the gas pedal and let the car glide to a halt. It is not uncommon to see drivers behind me change lanes, accelerate, and overtake me only to brake a few hundred feet later at the red light. I wonder if they know that such sudden acceleration and braking can use up to 30 percent more fuel. It is also not uncommon to see people driving way past the speed limits. They not only pose a threat to themselves and others but are also burning a hole in the ozone layer and their pocket. As a rule of thumb, you can assume that each five miles per hour you drive over sixty miles per hour is like paying an additional $0.20 per gallon for gas (assuming fuel price of $3.10/gallon). Other tips for driving more efficiently are as follows:[vii]

i. Minimize the use of air-conditioning.
ii. Minimize the weight of your car by removing any unnecessary stuff in your car. An extra one hundred pounds in your vehicle could reduce your mpg by up to two percent.
iii. Keep your windows shut especially if you are driving at high speeds.
iv. Minimize revving or idling of the engine. Idling gets 0 miles per gallon!

When I was living in Singapore, I did not own a car. In fact, I did not even have a driving license. I relied totally on public transportation. They have a good MRT (Mass Rapid Transit) system that is complemented with buses. If we had a good public transportation system here, I would not bother owning a car.

Space. I don't need that much because I don't have much stuff. You can also minimize your need for space by going paperless. If there is an option to sign up for e-statements, I sign up. Electronic statements not only spares the trees but also gives you the advantage of being able to view your records from anywhere you have access to a computer. There are also security concerns if your paper statement is not delivered properly and/or if you did not shred or dispose of it appropriately. If you are moving house, you don't have to worry about informing the banks on time, because you are getting everything electronically. Similarly, if there is an option to sign up for e-magazines or e-newsletters, I opt for that, too. How technology can help you in needing less space is discussed later.

When you don't need that much space, you don't need to buy a big house. You can live in a much smaller house. This translates to lower mortgage payments. Saving on your mortgage payments can drastically cut back on the number of years you need to work to pay off your mortgage. WL, a friend of mine, is looking to purchase a bigger house than I have because he thinks he needs the space. It is easily going to cost him at least $300,000 more than if he were to settle for a smaller space and in a less "prestigious" part of the county. How many more years will he have to work to pay the difference off? Most people try to buy the biggest house they can afford. They stretch themselves. Some overstretch. I took the opposite path. I did not go by what I could afford. As a minimalist, I went with the smallest place I could get. I did not go for a fancy or prestigious neighborhood. As such, my mortgage payments were relatively lower. What I saved on my primary residence, I diverted toward a rental property. So instead of buying one big property to live in, I bought two: one small place for myself to live in and another to rent out. The rent from my tenant was able to cover my mortgage payments on the rental property. As far as my residential property was concerned, I made mortgage payments instead of rental payments. You either pay rent or mortgage. I chose the latter. Contrary to what most financial advisors will advise, I did not maximize my 401(k). I maximized to get the employer match, but not more. Instead I diverted any extra dollars I had every month toward paying off my mortgage. From the earlier section, you will have realized that a minimalist does not have a lot of the recurring costs that most people have (cable, high electric bills, etc). All these savings were plowed toward paying off my mortgage sooner. Over time, I was able to pay off both my mortgages. I am debt free now. It was possible because of my minimalist lifestyle, not because I won a lottery or joined a start-up. Slow and steady wins the race! (Once again, financial advisors will say that paying off your mortgage is not a good idea and that we should maximize our 401(k). Believe me; I know all the cold analysis behind that advice. Only time will tell which was a better move for me.) The way I saw it was: A house is a tangible, physical asset. Regardless of whether the price goes up or down, people need to live somewhere. As such, you derive utility out of it regardless of its prevailing market price. With securities it is different. From March 2000 to Oct 2002, the S&P index value declined more than 49 percent and the NASDAQ fell over 77 percent. If that was the time you were retiring and you still had outstanding mortgage payments and other debts, what were you to do? If you don't need that money when the market is down, holding on to it does not yield you any utility like a physical asset such as a house does. The exception may be dividend-paying stocks. This is where the financial advisors would talk about the importance of diversification in your portfolio. Well, I consider the real estate that I own to provide that diversification. As long as you are paying mortgage, you don't own the house. The bank owns it. When you own your house outright, regardless of the state of the economy, you don't have to worry about the mortgage payments. Because you own your house, you are also shielding yourself from one aspect of inflation—rising costs of rent.

Healthcare costs. Prescription drugs: None. Over-the-counter medication: None. Yearly flu shots: None. In the last ten years, I have not taken any time off for illness. Yes, I have been blessed with good health and I am thankful for it. When you are truly thankful, you cherish it and this is why I am particular about my diet and lifestyle. I have always tried to stay away as much as possible from drugs, prescribed or otherwise. It is possible to live a drug-free life if one puts their heart and mind to it. Recall my story on how I brought down my cholesterol without resorting to statin. Unfortunately, people want quick fixes. They want a solution in a pill. Compound this with the fact that some doctors act like drug pushers peddling drugs. An *International Herald Tribune* article reported in 1997 that doctors were paid millions to push drugs which regulators now say may be unsafe at commonly used doses.[viii] Of course, not all doctors are guilty of this. We, however, need to take responsibility for our own health by paying close attention to our body and getting educated on some basic health matters. The following is worth remembering:

a. The adage: Prevention is better than cure. Diet and lifestyle decisions should be part of your prevention strategy. As such, be aware of what you eat. Be mindful of how and when you eat, too. In his latest book *In Defense of Food*, author Michael Pollan points out that most of what we're consuming today is not food. According to him, we're consuming no longer the products of nature but of food science. Hippocrates, the Father of Medicine, said, "Let food be your medicine and medicine be your food." He believed in the importance of good food and related the course of any ailment to poor nutrition and bad eating habits. He compiled a list of over four hundred herbs and their uses. It is ironic that today, resorting to herbs and spices as medicine is referred to as "alternative medicine." Shouldn't it be the other way around? Because herbs are naturally occurring and hence cannot be patented, drug companies have no motivation to fund any research that will prove that certain herbs may treat and even cure a disease. They instead concoct unnatural drugs that can be patented. Patented unnatural drugs may potentially make money for pharmaceutical companies (if the FDA approves it). Natural herbs don't.

b.   Sometimes the cure can be worse than the disease. I am sure you have heard of cases where a certain drug resulted in a patient's death.

When you work hard and consequently develop a headache, the headache is prompting you to take a break. It is a safety mechanism and your body is telling you to slow down. However, many people will ignore it. Some may even take medication such as Tylenol to numb their discomfort so that they can continue doing whatever they were doing. Think of it as the medication silencing the smoke alarm. Soon, people habitually take medication to numb the pain.

Early indicators are silenced. Eventually, a slightly more serious ailment develops. This time, a "stronger" medication is needed to treat the symptoms. Nothing is done to address the cause of the ailment. Once again, people continue on their medication regimen, ignoring and numbing any and all signals the body is giving them. This eventually culminates in something very major. If we take the time to listen to what our body tells us and address it promptly, we can avoid many problems down the road. Norman Cousins said, "The greatest force in the human body is the natural drive of the body to heal itself." Do you believe that?

Don't upgrade. One afternoon, when I was still living in Houston, Texas, my friend WK and I were off to a lunch in another part of town. He was driving my car since I was not familiar with that part of the town. (Yes, plus I don't like driving.) On the way back, he shook his head and commented that I was driving a piece of junk. He said that before I left for California, I should drive his Lexus to feel the difference. According to him, once I have driven a car of that caliber, I would never want to drive my junk again. I smiled and told him, "If that is the case, I will pass up on your offer." My rationale was as follows:

1. The primary purpose of my car is to bring me from point A to point B in the safest, reliable, and most cost-effective way possible. My Honda does that.
2. I am aware of the Diderot effect. I am also aware that my car insurance and gas costs are going to go up if I were to trade up. Gas costs would go up for two reasons: One is that I would probably have to fill it up with premium gas instead of regular gas. The other reason is reduced fuel

efficiency when compared to my current car. I am thinking not only of the initial price difference but the difference in the total cost of ownership over the lifetime of the car. The difference in cost if invested would yield better utility to me in years to come.

3. If I am satisfied with what I have, I don't bother trying to taste or try whatever is going to cost me more. Generally, if you don't have the willpower to resist the temptation to taste something, most likely you won't have the willpower to resist wanting more of it once you have tasted it. Selective ignorance is bliss. We can glide into an extravagant lifestyle easily. But to step down once you are used to that lifestyle is hard.

Eating out. I limit this to the minimum. Cooking your meals has the following advantages:

a. You get to choose the ingredients and the way it is cooked. Hence, it usually is healthier than what you can get at the restaurants.

b. The difference in cost can be significant. Over one's lifetime it can be hefty.

Group meals are an alternative to eating out. What I mean by group meals is where friends take turns to host dinners at their homes. When I do go out to eat, it is not uncommon for me to eat at an expensive restaurant if I deem the quality of food to be good.

Miscellaneous. I don't have or wear any rings or chains. I have one pair of jeans, one suit, one pair of dress shoes, one pair of sandals, one chopping knife, one saucepan, one pot . . . well, you get the idea. I tend to use them till I absolutely cannot salvage them any further before I discard or recycle them.

Finally, I also minimize the activities or routines that I engage in. Virtually all of my monthly bills I have put on autopilot mode by setting up automatic deductions from my checking account. I monitor my monthly e-statements carefully to ensure everything is correctly deducted. If you don't feel comfortable with autodeduct schemes, you may want to consider e-bill payments. It would at least save you writing a check or a making an extra trip to the mailbox.

I try not to be part of any group that I don't add value to. If necessary, I turn down invitations to social gatherings.

It has become quite common for people to multitask these days. Some even take pride in their ability to multitask. I came across the following on "Multitasking and Memory Loss" in a health statement from United Healthcare:

> A study at the University of Michigan suggests multitasking could actually be doing us more harm than good. People who spent time stopping and starting tasks took 2 to 4 times longer to complete them. In addition, brain scans showed juggling tasks reduces the brain power available for each. Over time, stress hormones from multitasking can damage memory centers in the brain. Focus on one task at a time for better efficiency and memory.

How many times have you been in teleconferences when someone asks you to repeat what you just said when they are asked a question?

Most likely they were multitasking. Perhaps you are guilty of it yourself. Our common excuse is that we have too much to do and so little time. So the way to accomplish all the tasks given the time constraints seems to be to multitask. The better alternative is to decline a responsibility if your plate is full. Yes, you may not be seen in a favorable light when it comes to performance reviews and when a promotion opportunity comes along. But years from now, you will at least still be sane. It is also better to complete a few tasks professionally than to be mediocre in multiple tasks.

Some of what I do may seem petty. It may be, but

1. small amounts saved and/or invested over time make a lot of difference and
2. apparently insignificant actions when practiced by many will have a huge impact on the society and the environment.

TRIVIA: American Airlines saved $40,000 in 1987 by eliminating one olive from each salad served in first class.

Key point: As trivial as it may seem, do not disregard the power of time and the power of the masses.

I encourage you to look at appendix D and consider the financial implications of your choices.

The acid test for me: If I become a billionaire tomorrow, would I still continue my way of life, like sleeping without a bed and not driving a fancy car? Unequivocally yes! Remember, it is not just about money. Just because you can afford something doesn't mean you should buy it. Each of us has to conscientiously think of the implications our every action has not only on our lives, but also how it affects the lives of others and the planet. You can expend your resources in indulging in yourself or you can consider nobler options. Check out appendix A.

Key point: Every decision we make not only has financial implications but also has social and environment considerations.

Take the minimalist challenge. See if you can best my daily usage. See if your daily usage can be below three kilowatts an hour.

Usage Table and History Graphs										
Service Type	Read Dates From To	Days	Meter Readings Current Prior		Mult	Usage	Meter Number	Rate	This Month This Year (Daily Avg)	This Month Last Year (Daily Avg)
E	02/06 03/04	27	17500	17460	1	40 kWh	24695	D1	1 kWh	2 kWh

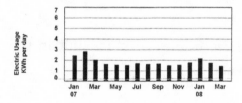

If you can achieve it; post it on www.youtube.com or report it in any blog or anywhere and wherever you can. Share how you did it and challenge other people to best your score. Let's see who "the minimalist of all" is.

> Nobody did worse than he who did nothing for fear he
> could only do a little. (Edmund Burke)

SOME AIDS FOR A MINIMALIST

Technology

My notebook computer is more than my computing device. It is my photo album, my CD player, my DVD player, my TV, and my (electronic) filing cabinet.

Years ago, I decided that I was going to digitize everything I had in paper. I started with my old photographs. I got them scanned and got rid of my physical photo albums. Following that, with the introduction of digital cameras, digital photos are what I take. I don't print any pictures. Next, I scanned all notes and articles I had saved and discarded the paper versions into a recycle bin. Any books I had, I either sold them or donated them. Whatever music I had in cassette forms, I got them converted to MP3 (or WMA) format and got rid of the cassettes. The CDs that I owned I ripped to my notebook computer. Following this exercise, I don't buy any more CDs. I just try to get the music or song that I like in the digital format (MP3 or WMA) and store them on my notebook computer. This is a good example of how you could increase your upr (utility per resource). Because you are using one resource (notebook computer) instead of multiple resources (CD player, DVD player, photo album) to achieve similar utility, your upr obviously improves. It also saves you space.

You can minimize what you have. All of the functions on the left can be performed by a notebook computer. You get to minimize your overall cost, space and carbon footprint. It also provides you convenience and mobility.

TV

DVD player

CD Player

Photo album

Filing cabinet

Fire is a good servant but a bad master.

The above proverb is generally true with almost anything, including technology. The challenge for us is to remain in control. We have to be in the driver's seat and decide when to utilize technology to our advantage and not let it control us. I try to keep abreast of what technology has to offer and am very selective on what I choose to adopt. Even when I chose to adopt, I am very conscientious (or at least try to be) about how much I want to be entrenched in it. When we choose to capitulate certain tasks to technology, over time we run the risk of losing our faculties.

Also, never assume that newer technology will always be better than older technology. In May 2005, on "The Tonight Show with Jay Leno," two Morse code men were able to beat a pair of teenaged text messengers equipped with modern cell phones. This victory replicated a similar challenge that took place in Australia. Imagine a 70-year-old beating modern technology.

Public Library

> I have always imagined that Paradise will be a kind of library. (Jorge Luis Borges)

I am a heavy user of the public library. I see it to be the best use of our tax dollars. Here are some benefits:

1. It helps you be a minimalist. You don't have to own any of the books you want to read. You can always borrow from the library.
2. Saves you money since you do not have to buy books, CDs, or movies.
3. Helps you to read, watch, or listen to whatever you wanted to read, watch, or listen to within a prescribed time. Because there are due dates, you are "forced" to spend time doing something that you wanted to do anyway.
4. It educates you through talks or classes they conduct.
5. It provides an avenue for you to donate your used reading materials, videos, CDs, and even art pieces.
6. It provides an avenue for you to volunteer.
7. It increases the utility per resource (upr) of the city. When a single resource like a book is utilized by several people over the lifetime of the book, the aggregate utility is significantly higher than a book sitting on someone's bookshelf at home and utilized by only that household.

The richest person in the world—in fact all the riches in the world—couldn't provide you with anything like the endless, incredible loot available at your local library. (Malcolm Forbes)

Like-minded Individuals

Although at the time of writing I am yet to be part of the Simple Living Network or its communities, the support the network provides can be useful for someone considering becoming a minimalist or who is already one but feels they are swimming against the tide. It provides a good avenue for people to share information, to give and get help.

COUNTERARGUMENT

Counterargument 1: It's the Economy, Stupid!

Critics of the minimalist lifestyle will pontificate that if everyone were to live like I do, our Gross National Product (GNP) would be affected. My response is as follows:

Firstly, let's be brutally honest. Regardless of how convincing my arguments are for the minimalist way of life, the vast majority will continue living their lives as they have been. Only a few will conscientiously choose to lead a simple life.

Secondly, if by an amazing grace the majority converts to become minimalists, that does not necessarily mean the GNP of a country is going to be affected. Let's be crystal clear first on how GNP is calculated:

$$GNP = C + G + I + NX + NFP \text{ where}$$

- C is the actual consumption spending of the household sector. It consists of food, clothing, and all consumers' spending.
- G represents goods and services. These items include salaries for government employees, national defense, and state and local government spending.

- *I* is for investment spending and it includes inventory spending; capital improvements and building machinery are included in this category. Investment in housing construction is also included.
- The net exports (NX) component is equal to exports (goods and services purchased by foreigners) minus imports (goods and services purchased by domestic residents).
- Net factor payments (NFP) are the net amount of payments an economy pays to foreigners for inputs used in producing goods and services—less money the economy receives for selling the same factors of production.

It is no secret that the U.S. economy is overdependent on consumer consumption to keep the GNP growing. Consumer spending is by far the largest component of our GNP and accounts for approximately two-thirds of the economy. Is this good? Is this the way you want the country to continue? We can be a nation of minimalists and still keep our GNP healthy by improving other factors that affect GNP such as the following:

- *G* for government spending. How about increasing necessary government spending on repairing bridges and enhancing levee systems? I emphasize *necessary*.
- *I* for investment spending. How about businesses increasing their business spending to improve the ability to produce in the future, or increasing investments in capital improvements?
- NX or Net exports. Isn't it about time we start to export more than we import? If we can achieve that, then we can certainly improve our net exports and consequently our GNP.

As you can see, minimalism will not bring the economy down. On the contrary, the true risk to the economy is a nation of citizens addicted to overconsumption. By cutting back on any wasteful personal consumption, the minimalist saves money that can then be made available for investments. The minimalist is in a position to direct his or her capital where it will earn the best return. Innovative efforts directed to places where they will earn a good return eventually improves living standards.

Key point: Personal consumption is not the only lever we have to improve the GNP.

Finally, we should ask ourselves if GNP is the right measure or the only measure we should be obsessed about. Robert Kennedy made the following remarks on GNP, I believe, at the University of Kansas on March 18, 1968:

> Too much and for too long, we seemed to have surrendered personal excellence and community values in the mere accumulation of material things. Our Gross National Product, now, is over $800 billion dollars a year, but that Gross National Product—if we judge the United States of America by that—that Gross National Product counts air pollution and cigarette advertising, and ambulances to clear our highways of carnage. It counts special locks for our doors and the jails for the people who break them. It counts the destruction of the redwood and the loss of our natural wonder in chaotic sprawl. It counts napalm and counts nuclear warheads and armored cars for the police to fight the riots in our cities. It counts Whitman's

rifle and Speck's knife. And the television programs which glorify violence in order to sell toys to our children. Yet the gross national product does not allow for the health of our children, the quality of their education or the joy of their play. It does not include the beauty of our poetry or the strength of our marriages, the intelligence of our public debate or the integrity of our public officials. It measures neither our wit nor our courage, neither our wisdom nor our learning, neither our compassion nor our devotion to our country, it measures everything in short, except that which makes life worthwhile. And it can tell us everything about America except why we are proud that we are Americans.

Hmm, clearly GNP seems to be an incomplete measure. If the above was not convincing enough, let me offer you another example: Say you were diagnosed with cancer and have to receive medical treatment. The cost you incur for the medical treatment helps the GNP. In fact (assuming you continue to work), the more expensive and long-drawn your treatment, the better it is for the GNP (or the economy). It is a cost and personal tragedy to you and to your family, but it is a benefit to the GNP. This is not a sick joke. It is a sad fact on how the GNP is calculated. So what is the alternative?

Consideration A. Have you heard about Green National Accounting? Green GDP Accounting refers to an accounting system that factors in natural resources depletion costs and environmental degradation costs to assess the quality of economic development in a real sense:

Green GDP = GDP—the costs of natural resource consumption—the costs of environmental depletion

The report titled "China Green National Accounting Study Report 2004" revealed that environmental pollution cost China 511.8 billion yuan (U.S. $63 billion) in economic losses in 2004. Although critics may caution about "Green GDP" and its methodological problems, one must also acknowledge how poorly represented sustainable development is in the existing way of looking at GDP. Shouldn't we be able to see how the market consumption affects clean air and clean water? Two popular green GDP systems are the Index of Sustainable Economic Welfare (ISEW) and the Genuine Progress Indicator (GPI). Appendix E provides an idea of the dollar value for the services and benefits provided by nature.

Consideration B. Have you heard about GNH? It stands for Gross National Happiness. The term was coined by the Bhutan king, Jigme Singye Wangchuck, in 1972 when he proclaimed GNH as the standard for the country's well-being. According to Wangchuck, economic growth does not necessarily lead to contentment. The four "pillars" of GNH are economic self-reliance, a pristine environment, the preservation and promotion of Bhutan's culture, and good governance. If the ultimate goal of any country's pursuit is the happiness of its citizens, then it may seem the GNH may be the right metric to pursue. Of course, there are criticisms of GNH. However, the concept is resonating with a wide range of initiatives across the world to define prosperity in broader terms that include the actual well-being of the people.

Key point: Don't be misled to think that GNP is the Holy Grail and that personal consumption is the only way to save it. There are other considerations, as discussed above.

Counterargument 2: This Lifestyle Is for Tree Huggers Only

Firstly, there should not be any ambiguity if there is global warming. That is the verdict of scientists. Climate change is just one consideration. The other consideration is the sustainability of natural resources. How long do you think the earth can continue to provide resources at the current growing rate of consumption? In the *Stern Review on the Economics of Climate Change*, the author, Sir Nicholas Stern, who is the head of the U.K. Government Economic Service makes a basic point unassailable: Failure to act now will exact much greater penalties later on. This is too important of a task to be left to just the tree huggers and minimalists. Everyone needs to do their part!

> Facts do not cease to exist because they are ignored.
>
> (Aldous Huxley)

Time for a short story. Tom and Dick were stranded on two different islands with no contact to the outside world. The island had identical resources:

- fresh water from a stream
- a reasonable number of chickens
- just the right number of fruit trees and greens
- a hut that provided adequate shelter

Dick, realizing there was no way out of the island, began to make the best use of it. Because the hens were easy to catch and kill and they seemed plenty, he just continued catching and killing them for meals whenever he felt like it. For fire, he indiscriminately chopped the trees. Out of boredom, he even started cock fighting.

Tom took a different approach. He realized that his survival depended on the survival of the chickens and the trees. He assessed carefully the number of chickens as well as the frequency they were laying eggs. He ate the chickens and the eggs in moderation so that there would always be enough chickens.

Weeks turned into months. One day, Dick began to panic. He only had few chickens and eggs left. He realized that he had to cut back. However, that did not come easy because he had gotten accustomed to eating sumptuously. Eventually he was left with no chickens or eggs. The fruit trees and greens were almost gone and whatever were left were not going to be bearing fruits for at least a couple of months. Just before one tree was going to bear fruit, Dick died of starvation. Tom continued to survive.

It is easy to dismiss the above as a fictional story. Fictional as it may, it should be no different from how we should consider the planet. The planet Earth is both a source and a sink. It is a source of sustenance to us. It is a sink because it absorbs all our waste. Has the planet gotten bigger? Has the population grown exponentially? If the planet has not grown bigger but the population has grown exponentially, how long can we keep mining the resources, chopping the trees, and overfishing the oceans?

How much garbage can your kitchen sink take before it begins to be dysfunctional? If it was designed for one family, how long could it keep functioning if it had to support ten families at one time? How much waste can we keep dumping into the seas and landfills? If we keep chopping all the trees, at what point would we realize we had chopped too many? Would we be like Dick, who realized it too late?

Financial advisors will tell you that the key to making retirement savings last lies in the withdrawal rate. If you withdraw too much, you may exhaust your savings. In what has become known as the Trinity Study, three professors from Trinity University in San Antonio, Texas, studied actual historical stock and bond returns to determine sustainable withdrawal rates. There have been several debates since then around the safe withdrawal rate. The rate often cited is 4 percent. So if you withdraw more than 4 percent, at some point you will end up running out of money. Like Dick, you may die of starvation. If we accept this notion of a safe withdrawal rate when it comes to financial resources, why do we find it so hard to apply the same principle to our natural resources? Why do we naively think we can just keep plundering the earth, fishing the oceans, and chopping the trees without restraint and that there will still be an endless supply of nature resources?

In 1956, M. King Hubbert predicted that U.S. oil production would peak in the early 1970's. At that time, he was widely criticized by some oil experts and economists. In 1971 Hubbert's prediction came true. Based on Hubbert's methods, when do you think we will reach a peak in world oil production? Feel free to do your own research by searching for terms such as "peak oil" or "Hubbert's Peak." Once you reach the peak, the remaining oil becomes increasingly costly to extract and refine.

Counterargument 3: You Cannot Be Happy Being a Minimalist

Doubtful that you can still be happy by minimizing? Of course, you can! You just have to recognize what you have and enjoy it. For example, part of my happiness hinges on the fact that I am blessed with good health. I have good family and friends. This gives me a lot of reasons to be thankful and happy. I don't have a 42-inch flat panel high-definition TV. However, I take pride in my 120-inch high-definition view from my home of the mountain range. I get to see the sun rise every morning and moon rise every month (assuming clear weather). I enjoy hearing the birds chirping in the morning. During the day, I enjoy watching the seagulls gliding so gracefully up in the sky. Once in a while, I get treated with a brilliant morning sky that is almost unbelievable. I truly cherish these and get immense joy out of them. They do not cost me a dime. No resources drained from the planet.

Go back to your answer on the "camping" question. If a minimalist lifestyle during camping yielded so much joy to you, why burden yourself with what other people think are necessities, which in reality are not? Take time to list down everything that money cannot buy that you enjoy today. Jot them down below.

Key point: Best things in life are free. Identify and enjoy them.

Counterargument 4: What Would My Friends and Other People Think of Me?

Great spirits have always encountered violent opposition from mediocre minds. (Albert Einstein)

Should we be guided by our moral compass or should we attempt to appease public opinion? Perhaps this Aesop fable may help. It is called "The Man, the Boy, and the Donkey."

A man and his son were once going with their donkey to market. As they were walking along by its side, a countryman passed them and said: "You fools, what is a donkey for but to ride upon?"

So the man put the boy on the donkey and they went on their way. But soon they passed a group of men, one of whom said: "See that lazy youngster, he lets his father walk while he rides."

So the man ordered his boy to get off, and got on himself. But they hadn't gone far when they passed two women, one of whom said to the other: "Shame on that lazy lout to let his poor little son trudge along."

Well the man didn't know what to do, but at last he took his boy up before him on the donkey. By this time they had come to the town, and the passersby began to jeer and point at them. The man stopped and asked what they were scoffing at. The men said: "Aren't you ashamed of yourself for overloading that poor donkey of yours—you and your hulking son?"

The man and boy got off and tried to think what to do. They thought and they thought, till at last they cut down a pole, tied the donkey's feet to it, and raised the pole and the donkey to their shoulders. They went along amid the laughter of all who met them, till they came to Market Bridge, when the donkey, getting one of his feet loose, kicked out and caused the boy to drop his end of the pole. In the struggle the donkey fell over the bridge, and his fore-feet being tied together, he was drowned.

"That will teach you," said an old man who had followed them:

"Please all, and you will please none."

Buckminster Fuller said, "You never change things by fighting the existing reality. To change something, build a new model that makes the existing model obsolete." By changing how we lead our own lives (as Mahatma Gandhi said, "You must be the change you want to see in the world") slowly but surely, other people would begin to realize there are alternatives. As the lifestyle of excesses begins to crumble, people would begin to revert to the basics. Being the "pioneer" or the odd one out takes courage.

GOING OVERBOARD

Is there a danger of oversimplification or trying to minimize something that should not be minimized? Yes, there is that possibility. In my case, I will indicate exercise as a good example. The common advice we hear or read is to exercise a total of at least thirty minutes on most or all days of the week. Initially, I resisted that advice, rationalizing that I am different. As a result, I never really exercised. I minimized by exercise to virtually zero.

I have never been fond of exercise. I always found it a chore. My poor vision also made me bad in sports. As such, I did not play any sports and hence did not get to exercise through sports, either. I thought if I watched what I eat (which I am generally good at), I didn't really have to exercise—or at least exercise as much as what we are supposed to. My exercise was minimized to daily routines such as

- taking the stairs instead of the elevator,
- cleaning my own house instead of relying on maids, and
- walking instead of driving whenever possible.

Obviously, the above were not sufficient. Nature has designed us and necessitates us to keep moving. If we don't, we suffer the consequences. My experience with my cholesterol levels that I shared earlier is a good example of how increased exercise together with appropriate change in diet helped reduce my cholesterol level.

However, overexertion also has its ill effects. Finding the right balance can be elusive. I have yet to determine what the optimum level of exercise is for me given my physique, diet, lifestyle, age, heredity, etc.

I am fully aware that my minimalist attitude may relegate me to sloth. That is something I have to constantly be vigilant about. If I don't, I know I can always depend on my critics to keep me on my toes.

CLOSING THOUGHTS

For those who believe in the merits of the minimalist lifestyle, I hope you will help spread the message in whatever way you can. I am not a leader. Nor am I a follower. I am more like a lone ranger. My value is in demonstrating, through my personal life, that one can still be happy despite being a minimalist. Unlike me, you may be a charismatic leader or you may be a popular blogger. Whatever you may be, I hope you help disseminate the merits you have read about.

For those who say that I cannot be truly happy being a minimalist, I offer the following:

I have lived the "normal life." I was last working for a Fortune 500 company in a fairly senior position. I used to have a furnished home. My first car was actually a sport convertible. I voluntarily switched and have been living the life of the minimalist for several years now. I deliberately chose to lead a simple and humble life well below my means. I find the latter much better. Since I have lived my life on both sides of the camp, it gives me some authority in saying which life is better—at least for me.

If you are not living the life of a minimalist, I encourage you to give it a try. Remember that a minimalist lifestyle does not mean no spending or limited spending. Instead, it is spending the minimum resources needed to reach the optimum point beyond which you divert those resources elsewhere to yield better returns or utility.

Several benefits have been identified in this book. You virtually have no risk in giving it a try. On the flipside, I cannot find a single benefit to support unbridled consumption or thoughtless spending. Of course, it is debatable if your spending is wasteful or purposeful. I hope the questions that I have posed will help you reexamine your assumptions. I urge you to examine your life and consider the implications of your lifestyle not just from the financial dimension but also the social and environmental impacts it may have on you and others down the road.

I challenge you to take the bold step in simplifying your life. Do it for your soul. Do it for the planet. If you don't believe in either of these, at least do it for your own health and your finances. At least give it a try. The experience will certainly prepare you for something else down the line.

The unexamined life is not worth living. (Socrates)

BEDTIME STORY

The following story "The Contented Fisherman" is from *The Song of the Bird* by Anthony de Mello.

The rich industrialist from the North was horrified to find the Southern fisherman lying lazily beside his boat, smoking a pipe.

"Why aren't you fishing?" said the industrialist.

"Because I have caught enough fish for the day," said the fisherman.

"Why don't you catch some more?"

"What would I do with it?"

"You could earn more money," was the reply. "With that you could have a motor fixed to your boat and go into deeper waters and catch more fish. Then you would make enough to buy nylon nets. These would bring you more fish and more money. Soon you would have enough money to own two boats . . . maybe even a fleet of boats. Then you would be a rich man like me."

"What would I do then?"

"Then you could really enjoy life."

"What do you think I am doing right now?"

RESOURCES

(S ome of these are not directly related to what was discussed in this book. I have found them either inspirational or educational. I have not listed the popular or obvious ones. Nor have I listed those already mentioned in the book.)

DVDs

To help illuminate you and get you to appreciate Mother Nature:

Planet Earth
The 11th Hour

To provide some insight into what we ingest:

Fast Food Nation
The Future of Food
How to Save the Planet

Directly or indirectly, we deal with big corporations. It is about time you understood them better:

The Corporation
Enron: The Smartest Guys in the Room

We are bombarded by media from the moment we wake up till the moment we retire to bed. Realize how they operate:

WMD: Weapons of Mass Deception
Orwell Rolls in His Grave

Books to consider reading

The man who does not read good books has no advantage over the man who can't read them. (Mark Twain)

The Precious Present by Spencer Johnson
Divine Interventions: True Stories of Mystery and Miracles That Change Lives by Dan Millman and Douglas Childers
The Road Less Traveled by M. Scott Peck

Web sites

A service that can help cut off junk mail almost completely: www.greendimes.com

An appliance energy use calculator can be found at this site: http://siliconvalleypower.apogee.net/homesuite/calcs/appcalc/

Carbon footprint calculator:
http://www.carbonfootprint.com/calculator.aspx

Retirement calculator:
http://moneycentral.msn.com/retire/planner.aspx
www.firecalc.com

You get to see here presentations from the world's leading thinkers
and doers:
http://www.ted.com/talks

An independent charity evaluator:
http://www.charitynavigator.org/

Allows whistleblowers to publish sensitive documents anonymously
on the Web:
www.wikileaks.org

APPENDIX A

In ancient China, foot binding was a practice. In modern times, we have "progressed" from fetish for tiny feet to big breasts and beefcakes. How much do you reckon women spend every year to make their breasts appear bigger? Just like how we look back at ancient China and shake our heads at their mindless practice, when will people look at our current fascinations and shake their heads?

I got the following information from http://worldcentric.org/stateworld/consumption.htm:

1. Currently, 80 percent of the world's resources are used by a minority of the world's population (17 percent).
2. Land, water, forests, etc., are exploited and used for producing goods and services for a minority of the world's population instead of being used to provide the basic necessities of food, water, health, sanitation, etc., for the rest of the world's population.
3. In order to fulfill the consumption "wants" of the rich minority, precious resources are often directed toward frivolous or luxury items, further depriving the poor of the world.

The site cites a table from Worldwatch Institute, which compares expenditures on luxury items with funding needed to meet basic needs. Below are some examples to put things in perspective:

Annual expenditure on pet food in Europe and United States = $17 billion

Additional annual investment needed to eliminate hunger and malnutrition = $19 billion

Annual expenditure on makeup = $18 billion

Additional annual investment needed to achieve clean drinking water for all = $10 billion

Annual expenditure on perfumes = $15 billion

Additional annual expenditure needed to gain universal literacy = $5 billion

Growing Disparity

The source for the next three charts in this appendix is the Institute for Policy Studies and United for a Fair Economy.

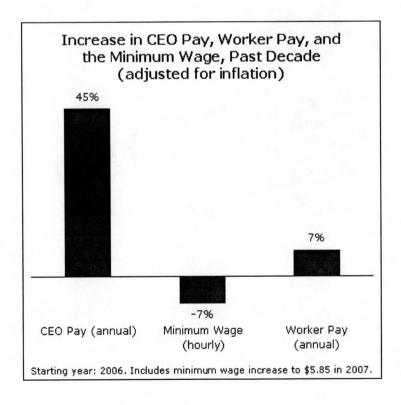

Source: Institute for Policy Studies and United for a Fair Economy.

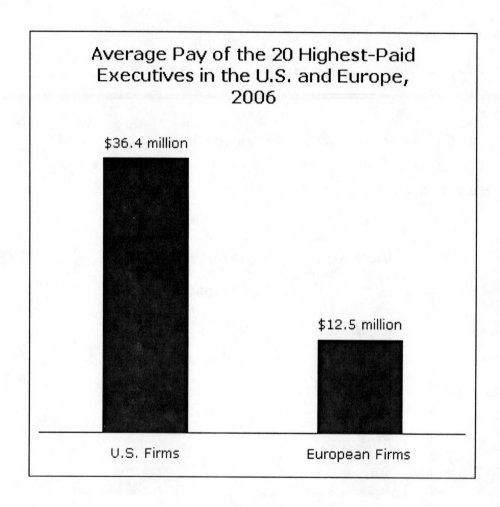

Source: Institute for Policy Studies and United for a Fair Economy.

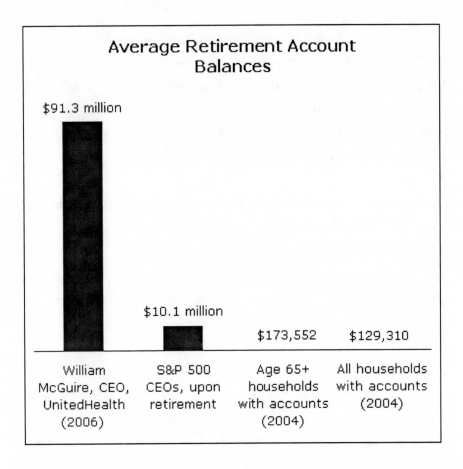

Average Retirement Account Balances

$91.3 million

$10.1 million

$173,552 $129,310

| William McGuire, CEO, UnitedHealth (2006) | S&P 500 CEOs, upon retirement | Age 65+ households with accounts (2004) | All households with accounts (2004) |

Sources: CEOs: Corporate Library, cited by Reuters and CNNMoney.com, June 11, 2007; Average Americans: Congressional Research Service analysis of the most recent Federal Reserve Board Survey of Consumer Finances.

The gap between the top and the rest has grown so much that the top 1 percent are paying almost 40 percent of all income tax (based on 2005 tax returns). This growing gap between the top and the majority is not good for *anyone*. The shrinking minority will end up paying most of the taxes and they will resent it. On the flipside, you have the bottom 50 percent paying nothing, or close to nothing, who resent those with higher incomes. Social cohesion falls apart once it hits the tipping point. What is the alternative? Some companies like Whole Foods Market have devised salary caps. The salary cap is a limit on total cash compensation paid to any team member in any calendar year. Employee benefits, stock options, and noncash 401(k) contributions are not counted in determining and applying the salary cap.

I got the information below from a press release that Whole Foods Market did on November 2, 2006 in http://www.wholefoodsmarket. com/investor/pr_06-11-02.html.

The following is the salary cap calculation for the company's past eight years:

Year	Average Hourly Wage	Annual Wage	Average Multiple	Salary Cap
1999	$12.36	$25,709	10	$257,000
2000	$12.84	$26,707	14	$373,900
2001	$13.46	$27,997	14	$391,900
2002	$13.69	$28,479	14	$398,700
2003	$14.07	$29,266	14	$409,700
2004	$14.66	$30,493	14	$426,900
2005	$15.00	$31,200	14	$436,800
2006	$15.38	$31,990	19	$607,800

Additionally, the company announced that John Mackey (CEO of Whole Foods Market) will reduce his salary to $1 beginning January 1, 2007, and forgo any future stock option award.

Credit Union versus Other Financial Institutions

Credit Unions	Other Financial Institutions
Not-for-profit	For profit
Owned by members: 1 member=1 ownership stake	Owned by shareholders. Shareholders can purchase high percentage that can drive decisions of management
Operated by mostly volunteer boards	Controlled by paid boards
Focus: Great service at a great price with low fees—for the benefit of membership	Focus: Profit maximization for the benefit of shareholders

1) The above are just the differences I was able to gather and tabulate. Feel free to do your research and arrive at your own decision.

2) The following site shows quite nicely the difference between banks and credit unions: *http://www.youngfreealberta.com/blog/ the-difference-between-banks-and-credit-unions-part-one*

A Penny Saved Is a Penny Earned

The most powerful force in the universe is compound interest. (Albert Einstein)

One important fact about compounding is that a small increase in the rate of return can produce a huge impact over time.

The other fact is that if instead of just making a one-time saving or investment, if you can save a certain amount every month and invest that every month, the impact becomes even greater.

How to interpret the table below: If your savings goal is $500,000 and if you only save $522 a month, it will take you twenty-five years to reach your goal. You can reduce the time taken to ten years if you save $2,715 a month.

The table below assumes 8 percent return compounded monthly. It does not factor in taxes.

Years needed/Your savings goal	$500,000	$750,000	$1,000,000
25	$522	$783	$1,045
20	$843	$1,265	$1,686
15	$1,435	$2,153	$2,871
10	$2,715	$4,072	$5,430

If the above amount is too much to save on a monthly basis, starting with $0 and depositing $100 monthly over 10 years (at a rate of return 8 percent compounded monthly), you will save $18,012. Again, it does not factor in taxes.

Value of Services Provided by Nature

The information below was obtained from http://pubs. usgs.gov/circ/c1172/table.html.

Ecologists and economists have collaborated to begin placing dollar values on a vast array of benefits and services provided to humans by ecosystems. Estimates range from $3 trillion to $30 trillion per year. Typical ecosystem services include fish provided by the sea, feed for cattle provided by grasslands, and tropical hardwoods provided by forests. This table exemplifies one attempt to place a price on nature and provides a basis for understanding the tradeoff that must be made when a wetland, for example, is destroyed.

Ecosystem*	Area (million ha)**	Value ($/ha/yr)	Global value ($trillion/yr)
Open ocean	33,200	252	8.4
Coastal	3,102	4,052	12.6
Tropical forest	1,900	2,007	3.8
Other forests	2,955	302	.9

Ecosystem*	Area (million ha)**	Value ($/ha/yr)	Global value ($trillion/yr)
Grasslands	3,898	232	.9
Wetlands	330	14,785	4.9
Lakes and rivers	200	8,498	1.7
Cropland	1,400	92	.1
Total worth of the biosphere			**$33.3**

* Desert, tundra, urban, and ice/rock ecosystems are omitted.
** Area in hectares (ha); 1 ha=100 square meters =2.471 acres.

Self-evaluation

Hopefully, by now you are motivated to take some action. The table below is to help record your current state of affairs and the changes you would see later. For example, if one of the things you decide to do is cut your electricity costs, you would note down your current usage as well as your monthly average bill in the "now" column. After several months, once you have executed the changes—like changing your lamps and removing phantom loads—you will note down the new values in the "after" column. The "Comments" column is for you to jot down your own notes. The more you choose to do and the more you can improve on will get you closer to financial independence, better health, and a better planet for all. Ironically, if there is one instance where more is better, it is in becoming more minimalist!

	Now	After	Comments
Your weight			
Time it will take to pack your essentials and go			
Number of incandescent bulbs in your house			
Carbon footprint (tonnes of CO_2)			

Daily consumption			
Food intake (calories)			
Hours spent watching TV			
Monthly expenditure			
Electricity usage (kWh)			
Electricity bill	$	$	
Water bill	$	$	
Prescribed drugs	$	$	
Over-the-counter medication	$	$	
Cable/satellite dish	$	$	
TiVo	$	$	
Telephone bill (landline)	$	$	
Cell phone	$	$	
Water filter	$	$	
Property tax on your home	$	$	
Home mortgage payments	$	$	
Car payments	$	$	
Car insurance	$	$	
Eating out	$	$	
Grocery bill	$	$	
Average monthly mileage (miles)			

Ethical Will

On Treating Yourself

1. My first goal in life is not to be a burden to myself and/or to society. My second goal is to help others not to be a burden to themselves and/or to society.
2. The less you depend on people and things for your happiness, the more you become your source of happiness.
3. Focus on things that really matter and those that you can add value to. Don't get distracted. Focus on your strengths and not on your weaknesses. An elephant is best in the forest and a camel best in the desert. No point for the elephant to spend time and energy trying to be like a camel. If it does, it will eventually end up being bad at both.
4. Avoid prescription drugs or over-the-counter drugs as much as possible. As the Father of Medicine said, "Let food be your medicine and medicine be your food." Be aware of what you ingest. Make every effort to eat real foods that are locally and organically grown and in season. Avoid GM (genetically modified) foods at all cost.
5. Mother Nature is self-healing. Give nature a chance to heal itself. Think about it: When you have a wound and the doctor dresses it, who or what actually heals the wound?

6.   No one culture, race, or religion has the answer to everything. You are usually better off in combining the best of what each has to offer and developing a style that fits the situation best. Example: Bruce Lee became formidable by studying styles from more than one form of martial arts.

7.   Two wrongs don't make a right. It is very tempting to justify a wrong action by claiming that you did it for the greater good. A wrong is a wrong. A lie is a lie, white or otherwise. Your yes should mean yes and your no should mean no.

8.   Don't make any decision out of fear, greed, pride, or anger.

9.   Get out while you are still ahead. Don't be greedy. Cut your losses as soon as you realize your decision is wrong. No point hanging on to bad investments hoping they would turn around, or worse still, injecting more resources into a lost cause. There is an opportunity cost to hanging on to bad decisions. Pumping more resources into a bad investment is tantamount to letting good resources chase after bad investments.

10. Don't compare your life with others. You have no idea what they may have gone through in life. You don't know what is in store for you or for them. Each of us has our own unique role to play and there is no backup. When we fail to recognize our true vocation and live it, we are doing a disservice to ourselves and to others. As Abraham Maslow said, "A musician must make music, an artist must paint, a poet must write if he is to be ultimately at peace with himself."

11. Always take some time to be alone to reflect things through. If possible, take a hike to the mountains or to a water source. If that is not possible, spend time quietly with nature.

12. Recognize all the good things you have and be thankful.

13. Nothing lasts forever. If you are going through bad times, just remember that no storm lasts forever.

On Treating Others

1. Mother Nature is forgiving. So follow nature: Try to forgive others as soon as possible. It is not always easy, but holding a grudge only does you more harm than good.
2. When you have the opportunity to help someone, help. Don't keep tabs on who you helped. Just help. Don't help expecting something back. Just help. Amazingly, you will get the help when you need it most (not necessarily from the same people you helped).
3. When you are not sure if you should go the extra mile to help someone, ask yourself what you would want if the roles were reversed.
4. We are only asked to love our neighbor as much we love ourselves. No more. No less. Usually, we end up either overextending ourselves or loving ourselves too much—meaning we become too obsessed with our own happiness, impervious of the consequence that has on others.

There is a common cliché "Money doesn't buy happiness." Many people just repeat this like a parrot. As long as we are not living in a barter-based economy, money can buy happiness. But the following points are also true:

* Money can also buy sorrow.
  o Money can lead to sorrow if used in the wrong way. A truly happy person judiciously uses his money

to procure only what he needs to secure happiness. A fool spends his money on frivolous wants and suffers later.

* The way one goes about getting money can result in sorrow.
   o The happier people are those who do what they enjoy to earn money and use the money wisely to procure only the things they need. Others compromise their principles and health in their pursuit of money and consequently negate the happiness they were after.
* Money is not the only thing that can bring us happiness.
   o There are other things that contribute to our happiness besides money, such as a clear conscience, mental and physical health, and endearing relationships.
* The best things in life are free—no money is needed.

A happy person is the one who realizes all the above points and is able to achieve them.

ENDNOTES

i   We need six planets:
http://marketplace.publicradio.org/display/web/2007/11/09/consumed1_pm_2/#

ii   Trees for newspapers:
I got this information from *National Geographic*'s Web site. They have a program called "Human Footprint."

iii   Junk mail and carbon dioxide:
http://magazine.continental.com/200804-the-guide

iv   Flame retardants. Check video on this site
http://cbs5.com/local/consumer.watch.flame.2.661700.html

v   Superior underwater vision in humans:
http://www.lu.se/vision-group/people/alumni/anna-gislen

vi   Traffic deaths on U.S. roads:
http://www.consumeraffairs.com/news04/2007/05/highway_deaths.html

vii   Driving more efficiently:
http://www.fueleconomy.gov/feg/driveHabits.shtml

viii   Doctors get paid millions by drug companies:
http://www.iht.com/articles/2007/05/09/business/anemia.php

INDEX

H

happiness, 23, 41, 69, 73, 98, 100
Hubbert's Peak, 73
hurricane Wilma, 49

I

In Defense of Food (Pollan), 54
Intergovernmental Panel on
    Climate Change, 28
IPCC. *See* Intergovernmental
    Panel on Climate Change
Iroquois law, 28
ISEW (Index of Sustainable
    Economic Welfare), 69

K

Kawashima, Ryuta, 45
Kennedy, Robert, 67
Kinder, George, 24

L

law of diminishing marginal
    utility, 15
Longevity Diet, The (Delaney and
    Walford), 32
Lost Horizon, 19, 26

M

"Man, the Boy, and the Donkey,
    The" (Aesop), 74
Max-Neef, Manfred, 41
McCandless Chris, 17
minimalism, 67
minimalists, 15, 28, 40, 52, 67,
    70, 78
  aids to, 61
  challenge, 60
  definition of, 13
  lifestyle, 16, 28, 65, 73
  reasons to be, 26
  two misconceptions on, 13
money, 14, 24, 30, 39, 41, 45,
    53, 55, 60, 63, 66, 73, 80,
    100
multitasking, 58

N

needs, 19, 24, 28
notebook computer, 31, 43, 61

O

obesity epidemic, 27

P

peak oil, 72
phases, 34, 36, 38
Pollan, Michael
  In Defense of Food, 54
public library, 44, 63

Q

quotes, 18, 26

S

safe withdrawal rate, 72
salary caps, 90
"Soak up the Sun" (Crow), 18
Song of the Bird, The (De Mello),
  80
Stern Review on the Economics of
  Climate Change (Stern), 70
Stern, Nicholas
  Stern Review on the Economics of
  Climate Change, 70
Surin islands, 48

T

Taos Pueblo, 31
"threshold hypothesis", 41
Tonight Show with Jay Leno, The,
  62
tree huggers, 70
Trinity Study, 72

U

underwater vision, 48
universal physical needs, 23
upr (utility per resource), 15, 34,
  40, 61, 63
"use it or lose it", 31

W

Waldfogel, Joel, 14
Wangchuck, Jigme Singye, 69
wants, 20, 24, 32, 85, 101
Worldwatch Institute, 86

Printed in the United States
144429LV00002B/11/P

9 781436 348638